T0198907

GOD MADE ME PERFECT AND WONDERFUL

TO DO WHAT?

Written by
Icilda V. Hogan

Pictures by
Victor V. Hogan II

AuthorHouse™
1663 Liberty Drive
Bloomington, IN 47403
www.authorhouse.com
Phone: 833-262-8899

Because of the dynamic nature of the Internet, any web addresses or links contained in this book may have changed
since publication and may no longer be valid. The views expressed in this work are solely those of the author and do
not necessarily reflect the views of the publisher, and the publisher hereby disclaims any responsibility for them.

Any people depicted in stock imagery provided by Getty Images are models,
and such images are being used for illustrative purposes only.
Certain stock imagery © Getty Images.

This book is printed on acid-free paper.

ISBN: 978-1-4490-4545-6 (sc)

Print information available on the last page.

Published by AuthorHouse 04/21/2021

author HOUSE

All scriptures reference is paraphrased from the New King James, NIV and the Amplified versions of the Bible. Paraphrasing the scriptures makes it easier for children to understand and apply them to their lives.

Text © copyright 1999 by Author, Icilda V. Hogan
Photograph-illustration © copyright 2003 by Victor V. Hogan II

ISBN 978-0-9762182-0-3

DEDICATION
I dedicate this book with love to my eight precious grandchildren: Christian, Caelan, Maya, Zachary, Langston, Gabriel, Ella and Naomi who God made perfect and wonderful.

ACKNOWLEDGEMENT
I thank Victor I, my husband; Vanessa, my daughter; Terrance, my son-in-law; Asha my daughter-in-law; and Darcy, my cousin for their support and encouragement. Special thanks to Victor II, the illustrator, my anointed and talented son. And above all I thank my Heavenly Father for choosing me to write this book.

Dear Parents,

GOD MADE ME PERFECT AND WONDERFUL- *To Do What?* Is the sequel to God Made Me Perfect and Wonderful – *A Daily Devotional for Children*. This second book will help you encourage your child, at an early age, to know that he or she was created by God with a special purpose to fulfill.

Please take the time to lead your child to Jesus Christ by having them repeat the following prayer of salvation.

PRAYER OF SALVATION

GOD, I believe in my heart

And say with my mouth

That JESUS is Your Son.

I believe He died for my sin.

I believe You raised Him from

the dead, and He lives.

Jesus, please come into my heart

and save me.

Thank You, JESUS, for saving me.

God, before You took me out of my mommy's womb, You already knew the plans You had for me. (Psalm 71:6) God, please tell me the plan You have for me. (Jeremiah 1:5)

God, did You make me a musician?

God, did You make me a *soldier*?

God, did You make me a *fashion designer?*

God, did You make me an architect?

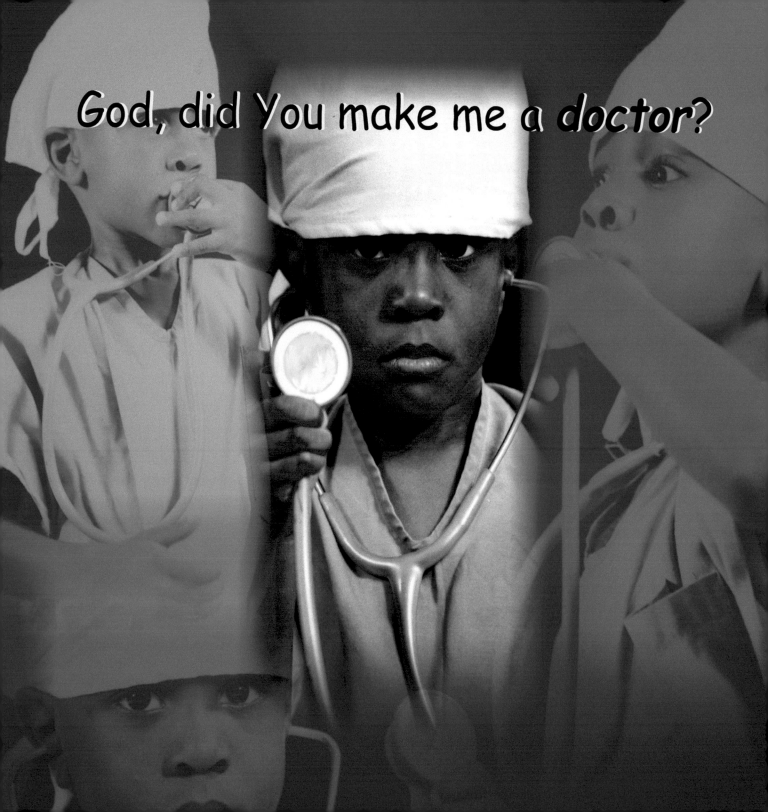

God, did You make me a *nurse*?

God, did You make me a *basketballplayer?*

God, did You make me an *artist*?

God, did You make me a *firefighter?*

God, did You make me a *policeman* or a *policewoman*?

God, did You make me a photographer?

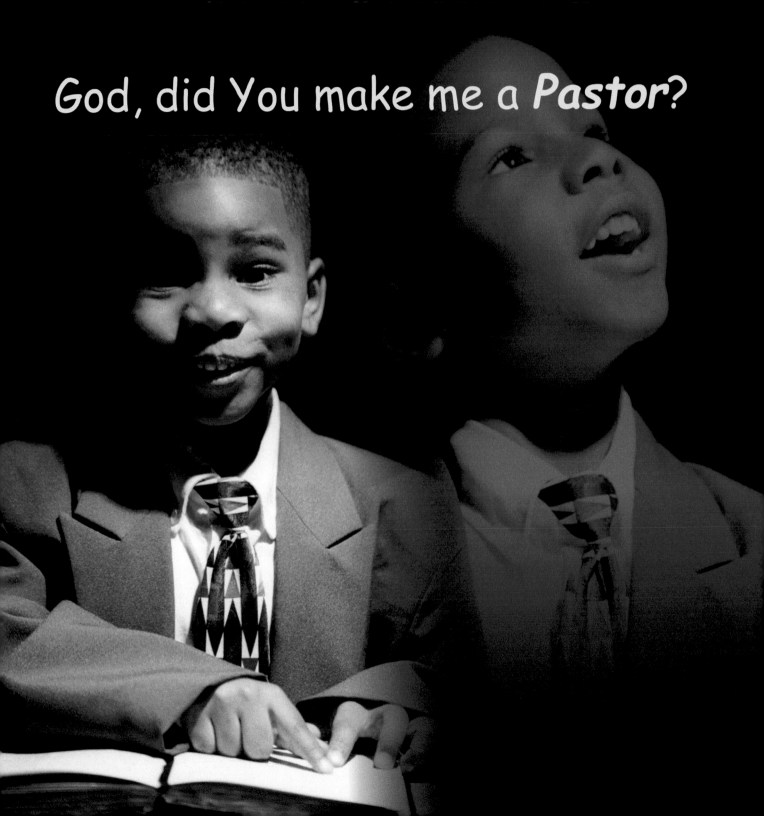

There is no one like me in this whole wide world. I am one of a kind.

God I praise You because You are wonderful. God I thank You for the wonder of my birth. (Psalm 71:7)

God, what did You created me to be?

About the Author

Icilda V. Hogan is a native of the Re-
public of Panama. After attending La
Boca Junior College, Icilda married
her high school sweetheart, Victor,
and migrated to the United States.
She and her family lived in New York
for many years and later relocated
to Atlanta where they presently live.
She and her husband have two children and eight grandchildren.

Icilda is a born again Christian who has a passion to see
children discover their God given purpose and destiny at
an early age. For many years, she worked with and taught
children of all ages from tots to teens. In addition, she has
served God in the church in many capacities as a Sunday
School and New Members' teacher, and a Young Women's
Missionary leader to name a few. Currently she serves as
Director, along with her husband, of the Community Group
Ministry at one of the largest and fastest growing churches
in the United States.